Yard

Rebecca Prichard was born in [...] she studied drama at Exeter University and graduated in 1993. Her plays include *Essex Girls* (Royal Court, 1994), and *Fair Game* (based on Edna Mazya's *Games in the Backyard*, Royal Court, 1997).

Rebecca Prichard
Yard Gal

faber and faber

First published in 1998
by Faber and Faber Limited
3 Queen Square London WC1N 3AU
Published in the United States by Faber and Faber Inc.
a division of Farrar, Straus and Giroux Inc., New York

Typeset by Country Setting, Kingsdown, Kent CT14 8ES
Printed in England by Mackays of Chatham plc, Chatham, Kent

A CIP record for this book
is available from the British Library

ISBN 0–571–19591–1

2 4 6 8 10 9 7 5 3

Yard Gal was written for Clean Break Theatre Company in association with the Royal Court Theatre, London. The play was premièred at the Royal Court Theatre on 7 May 1998, with the following cast:

Marie Amelia Lowdell
Boo Sharon Duncan-Brewster

Director Gemma Bodinetz
Designer Es Devlin
Lighting Design Tina MacHugh

Yard Gal received its American première at MCC Theater, New York (Robert LuPone and Bernard Telsey, artistic directors), on 26 April 2000.

Characters

Marie

Boo

Act One

Marie and Boo sit on stage staring at the floor avoiding the audience's stare. They psych each other out as to who will begin the play.

Boo Wha' you looking at me for?

Marie Uh?

Boo Wha' you looking at me for man?

Marie Ain't you gonna start it?

Boo I ain't starting it start what?

Marie Fuck you man, the play.

Boo I ain't tellin' them shit.

Marie What?

Boo I ain't tellin' them shit. If you wanna make a fool of yaself it's up to you. I ain't tellin' them shit.

Marie You said you's gonna back me up! You said you's gonna back me up tellin' the story.

Boo Is backing you up starting it?

Marie Is sitting there with a face like a slap arse backing me up? You're such a pussy Boo, you know that.

Boo Don't start calling me names Marie or I ain't doing this play at all.

Marie Cha.

Slight pause. Boo loses patience.

Boo (*aggressively*) This is a story about me and Marie and the posse that we used to move with. It's about chatting shit getting fucked, getting high and doing our crimes and the shit that be going down in the yard innit.

Marie Right.

Boo We's from Hackney. People talk a lot of shit about Hackney when they ain't never been there, and they talk a lot of shit about yards when they ain't never met none. So me and Marie we come to tell you a story that is FI' REAL. Innit Marie.

Marie Word.

Boo Everybody be chatting about the violence and the guns and drugs on the east sides, saying we should get out, but uh uh. No way. I don't leave my roots at all. That's what I was born and brought up with and that's what I stay with. I'm a rude gal. I'm a HACKNEY GAL! And wherever I go everybody knows I'm there. And nobody touch me nobody talk to me and nobody come near me 'cos they cross me they know my posse cut them up one time, y' arrright! YARD GAL WE A RUN TING! SAFE.

Boo sits down again.

Marie There was six of us innit.

Boo Yeah, then five.

Marie There was.

Boo There was.

Marie (*slowly*) Threse. She was in our posse. She was a white gal innit. Like me.

Boo Yeah. She was a wigger. And she was the mampee of our crew.

Marie   Which means there was 'nuff of her.

Boo   Plenty for them mans to get hold of.

Marie   She was big.

Boo   And she was bold.

Marie   Ya didn't wanna mess with that you get me.

Boo   We used to call her screwface innit, 'cos she never ever smile.

Marie   But once she get a drink or a spliff inside her she was alright.

Boo   And she could graft. All day every day she be out on the streets in her batty riders or her shorts smokin' up and getting high and graftin'.

Marie   And she could front. She just walk into shops pick up what she want and walk out.

Boo   Yeah man. I didn't like graftin' with her, she was too bold.

Marie   She was blatant.

Boo   She used to deal and she carry all her dope wrap up in her pussy. And when she want it she jus' reach inside her and take it out. Anywhere. Didn't matter. On the street. In a shop. Anywhere.

Marie   She was low man.

Boo   Yeah, I do that kind of shit in the toilet.

Marie   (*looks askance at Boo*) Yeah. (*then*) Police always be taking her down the station innit.

Boo   But she always get off.

Marie   She go 'Man, I give 'em licks. Them police are pussies. I kicked off at 'em – they tink they can mess with Miss T – they have to let me go just to get rid of me.'

Boo   There was a rumour about Threse that she got thrown out a window when she was five innit.

Marie   Yeah, and we tink she must have landed on her head.

Boo   'Cos she was nutty like that.

Marie   She was up for anything.

Boo   Any dare you give her she do.

Marie   First dare you have to do if you wanna be in our posse is have a tattoo weren't it.

Boo   That was painful innit.

Marie   You get a needle.

Boo   Nah, first you get stoned.

Marie   Or pissed.

Boo   Or pissed and stoned.

Marie   Then ya get a needle – prick the skin and rub in the ink.

Boo   Threse she had enuff tattoos. Pictures everytin'. I just have my name. Simple see 'Boo'. My real names Bukola. But that's what everyone calls me, 'Boo', see.

Marie   Show them the one on you arse as well.

Boo   Fuck you man. I ain't sitting up here to be made a fool of you know.

Marie   We sitting up here to tell a story innit.

Boo   Don't start ramping with me or I will just go.

Marie   Tell them about Deanne.

Boo What about Deanne?

Marie Deanne man. She was lovely innit.

Boo Yeah. She have a heart din't she.

Marie She was sort of womanly. Big tits but then a really babyface innit. Face like a five-year-old girl. She was about two years younger than us as well.

Boo Yeah you could chat any amount of shit to her and you almost start believing it yourself weren't it.

Marie She used to wear her hair all styled down straight.

Boo Then she started putting weaves in.

Marie Just to copy Sabrina.

Boo She used to say Sabrina was her sister.

Marie And Sabrina'd be like 'That cow ain't my sister. What she chatting shit for?'

Boo Sabrina was just vex that Deanne was always borrowing her clothes.

Marie One time Sabrina had all these gold weaves put in her hair. She chuck her old weave away.

Boo Next day Deanne's wearing it. We're like 'Deanne man, your hair looks beautiful.' She's like 'It's Sabrina's, I took it out the bin.'

Marie She didn't care. She just look up to Sabrina.

Boo She always need someone to look up to innit.

Marie She was from the kids' home. That's where Boo's from as well. I lived with me Dad.

Boo But most the time I go round Hackney, 'cos I hated it at the home. They call it a kids' home, but basically it was a nut-house. I was like fifteen and I couldn't wait to get out.

Marie Me and Sabrina and Threse we used to love going up there. We climb in through the windows at night. There was 'nuff drink and 'nuff gear there. You could get out ya box and nobody done nothing. The carers there they just see it as a job din't they.

Boo Yeah. Pay by the hour.

Marie When Boo first come to our school she never used to talk. People thought she was deaf and dumb.

Boo (*shrugs*) I just din't have nothing to say.

Marie She give everyone mad starey eyes like dis.

Boo Fuck you – I hated you when I first see you.

Marie Did ya?

Boo Yeah. We had a bad fight. I box you up and you tell me you have a rare blood type. Like when your nose bleeds it don't stop and you die.

Marie I took the piss out your shoes on the first day of school. We always knew who the kids from care was at school, 'cos they come in a big orange bus with 'London Borough of Hackney' on. And we used to throw shit at them and take the piss. But then me and Boo have a fight and we been best mates ever since.

Boo Yeah.

Marie Best mates from time.

Boo Yeah.

Marie We go everywhere together and we done everything together innit.

Boo Tha's right.

Marie The girls in the posse they even used to say we was a bit the other way. But we was just close.

Boo Yeah. They was just jealous man, 'cos none a' them have a best mate like Marie was to me.

Marie And none a' them have a mate like Boo.

Boo I used to be always knocking up for Marie and going round her house, 'cos I never like to be at the home. Shit was kicking off all the time. Windows broken for weeks, because chairs been thrown threw them. You had to like sleep with ten pee under ya pillow in case you want to call an ambulance . . .

Marie But that's another story.

Boo Is it?

Marie Yeah man. We ain't got time for all your sad stories about the home. This is a story about yard gals innit. Tellin' them how tings a run in a yard.

Boo Is it really.

Marie Don't start throwing a moody Boo.

Boo I ain't.

Marie Don't start showing me no bad face.

Boo Piss off you cow.

Marie Don't start rampin', we gotta do this play. Don't even go there.

Boo Well tell it then, it's your play, 'yard gal'.

Marie Fuck you.

Boo Tell them who else is in the posse.

Marie Ask nicely.

Boo Tell them about Sabrina.

Marie   Ya put me in a funny mood now.

Boo   Sabrina was kriss weren't she.

Marie   Yeah.

Boo   She go out with like five men at once, and she tief the livin' amount of clothes.

Marie   She wear hipsters –

Boo   Leggings –

Marie   Halter tops with sequins –

Boo   And she always look good innit.

Marie   Yeah.

Boo   She was skinny but all she eat was chips. Chips for –

Marie   – Breakfast, chips at night.

Boo   She was a chip.

Marie   But her legs go right up to her bum din't they.

Boo   And higher.

Marie   Everywhere she walk some bway be coming up to her going 'Sistah, ya looking fit star, sometin' haff happen between me and you.'

Boo   Most a' them boys was dogs though to them that know.

Marie   Most a' them was yard bways.

Boo   She ride around in their BMW convertibles, music busting their ear drum.

Marie   Them wearing them posh clothes – Moschino top and trousers.

Boo   Big gold chains.

Marie Gun, mobes.

Boo They all hang round Hackney, sweeting up girls, seeing who the youngest is they can get pregnant.

Marie Yeah they chat them up and friend them up a bit.

Boo Give them some drink.

Marie And gear on tick.

Boo They call them 'baby love'.

Marie And 'sweetheart'.

Boo Making them feel all grown up.

Marie Then the girl is like –

Together 'Oh Ranklin I think I wanna have your babies.'

Marie Then they're sucking cock for rock.

Boo They sweeting them up and fucking them but at the end of the day they always wanna put you to work.

Marie Sabrina though she weren't no airhead.

Boo She knew how to manners them bways.

Marie She was a dealer herself so she always get respec'.

Boo And she could fight man.

Marie Yeah. She fight with her feet 'cos she always be protecting her hair.

Boo She be like 'Bitch, I fight you. But don't be distressing my weave. Took me all day star, right?'

Marie She keep her drugs in her weave like that, innit.

Demonstrates tucking a wrap of gear into a weave.

Boo Yeah. And kick with her feet. (*demonstrates*)

Marie Our posse was always getting into fights man.

Boo Wendy and her posse they was always rampin' with us.

Marie Wouldn't leave us alone innit.

Boo Yeah. Wendy and her posse was a bunch of filthy slappers that work down Hackney station, and they used to front us saying we steal their punters and deal on their manor.

Boo But we don't steal their punters. We just do clippin', telling men we gonna love them up nice then two two's, takin' their money and going 'Laters,' innit.

Marie Yeah – you could make like two hundred quid a night shankin' like that.

Boo Until the police start sticking fines on you.

Marie There was one gavver down the station we got friendly with though innit.

Boo Me and Marie used to go in his car.

Marie We was just bored.

Boo And he was bored as well – so we keep him company innit.

Marie Plus his wife had just had a baby so she weren't up for no sex.

Boo So he pay for a bit on the side.

Marie I used to like going in his car.

Boo It was a laugh.

Marie I just like going in cars man.

Boo   But if we get too buzzed and start playing on his radio or shouting out the window he used to chuck us out.

Marie   So we had to hold it down and chill.

Boo   We used to talk to him like he's our mate.

Marie   That annoyed him innit 'cos he never knew if we was taking the piss.

Boo   He used to say he didn't wanna be a police officer no more and it weren't all that.

Marie   He used to feel proper sorry for himself.

Boo   And we feel sorry for him as well.

Marie   We used to walk up to his car and Boo'd be like 'You do his bottom half and I'll do his top half.'

Boo   And you'd be like 'Nah man! I'll take his top half and you do his bottom half.'

Marie   And then we fight over who sit in the front.

Boo   One time they done a big round up down the station and arrested us all – and kept us in overnight.

Marie   He was there near our cell. We kept askin' him to get us water or a pill but he just totally blanked us man.

Boo   He was out of order.

Marie   So we started shouting out his name, but he wouldn't talk to us.

Boo   We knew his dick was about three inches long – totally bald and had a bend in it.

Marie   We started shouting that out – but he still blanked us innit.

Boo   Next time we's in his car we got him back though.

Marie   Yeah man. I give him a long blow job then I bit him.

Boo   I's sitting in the back of his car and Marie's blowing him. He was getting right into it giving it 'mmm', 'aah', like that weren't he.

Marie   If you could of been there it would have made you sick.

Boo   I was stroking his head and trying to fuck about with the siren. He had his head leant back and he's giving it 'Mind if I come in your mouth?'

Marie   I felt like I'd been blowing him for years. Me ear kept knocking against the seat-belt holder. And me eyes was fucking watering where he was nearly sticking it down me throat.

Boo   I started kissing him, but it was alright 'cos I was sucking a mint for protection.

Marie   He was making me nearly faint where he had his hands pumping my head so's I couldn't stop. I felt like I was gonna be there for the rest of me life. So I took his prick between my teeth and bit him, hard as I could without biting it off. His head nearly hit the fucking roof of the car.

Boo   I was looking at Marie like 'What the fuck . . .' and it weren't her he slaps, it was me.

Marie   I didn't wait for nothing – I had me hand on the door already and we dust it out the car.

Boo   He was giving it 'You bit my dick you little slapper, you bit my dick.'

Marie   I goes 'Yeah and it was a small meal you cunt,' and we run off down the street.

Boo   He never took us for no more rides after that, did he?

Marie   We tell the girls about it later and Deniz just goes 'Should have took some money off him first you pussies.'

Boo   When it come to being a pro Deniz knew the score innit.

Marie   Deniz was tall.

Boo   And skinny like a rake – she wear leggings and her legs look like sticks.

Marie   Her face was old – she look about thirty, but she was fifteen like the rest of us.

Boo   Because she look old she could do bun and cheese.

Marie   Cheque-book and card.

Boo   She'd wear all granny clothes to go shopping in – she could get away with anything 'cos she look thirty.

Marie   I prefer tiefin' – I don't like all the front of cheque-book and card. You got to act.

Boo   Yeah tiefin' is simple – in and out, up front.

Marie   But Deniz was a good tief as well.

Boo   I never see her eat you know that.

Marie   She never eat that's why.

Boo   And she never sleep.

Marie   Her face be like quicksand innit. Nose and eyes slowly sinking in.

Boo   Ya hypin' it again man.

Marie   When she was in a mood she was like a shadow in a room. She have some weird science shit about her where people didn't really want to touch her.

Boo Even the police. Sometimes she disappear for weeks and we never know where she went.

Marie But she could be a laugh as well.

Boo Threse used to dare her to go and knock on people's doors and act like she's their relative.

Marie Some of them used to let her in as well – then we'd all pile in.

Boo Then we'd all be sitting round drinking tea going 'How's Sonia?'

Marie This really nice old lady let us in once. We was chattin' 'er up nice, feelin' right at home in her flowery chairs. Then 'er sister come out the back room.

Boo She was mean man. Have a face like a onion.

Marie She chase us with a stick going 'You black bastards, get out of this house!'

Boo Deniz was seein' a yardie as well, weren't she.

Marie Yeah man. He was bad. The only people 'e wouldn't kill is them that's already dead.

Boo And even then he think twice innit.

Marie We was never into yardies. But we was both seeing this one dealer.

Boo Nero.

Marie Nero live on the Edgbaston Estate in Hackney.

Boo 'E was a dread.

Marie 'E was a big warm smiley geezer.

Boo 'E 'ad a low key racket but 'e made a good living.

Marie 'E didn't mind other dealers on his turf 'cos he had his regulars who trust his gear and know 'e don't cut the product.

Boo   'E weren't into violence at all.

Marie   'E was a nat'ral lover bway!

Boo   A mystic lover!

Marie   Dem older men can love sweetly star.

Boo   I like to be with a man that know how to mek me feel good! You get me.

Marie   'E 'ave long dread and soft brown eyes.

Boo   'E dressed slack though.

Marie   Dirty T-shirt and tracky bottoms.

Boo   But it ain't the clothes it's the man underneath.

Marie   We used to go round and help him weigh up sometimes.

Boo   And help him smoke ganja.

Marie   Until we got tired of him speechin' us.

Boo   'E love his own voice didn't he.

Marie   Once he start speechin' that was it.

Boo   He'd be weighing up his gear going –

Marie   'Every step you take make sure you gain from it – no-one's gonna give you nothing.'

Boo   'Look at the youth roun' 'ere, none a them a' prosper.'

Marie   'Them just build a prison round themselves.'

Boo   'We have to find out our reality.'

Marie   'We have to create a equal society. Drugs is an evil that is keeping us down. Committing crime on our own doorstep.'

Boo 'E was always talking shit about making money and dealing to get out the area and speechin' us that we should 'n all, 'cos things can only get worse.

Marie We jus' nod, and sit back and smoke his weed.

Boo But most the time we spend with the girls.

Marie Just chattin' shit, sitting out on walls with a drink when the sun was shining and graftin'.

Boo Sometimes we spend whole days just getting out our box. And when we have money we go to clubs as well.

Marie Spend the whole afternoon getting ready.

Boo gets up and starts 'doing' Marie's hair.

Boo I do your hair and Threse does Deanne's. No-one does Deniz 'cos she don't like to be touched.

Marie And Sabrina 'as spent the whole day getting ready anyway.

Boo Pass me the hair-piece.

She parts her hair with a comb then starts to put on the long curly hair-piece with an elastic band, then gells the rest of her hair back – they talk throughout.

Marie I wanna look kriss man. All the rude bways gwan big me up tonight star.

Boo Ya too man crazy girl, innit.

Marie Deniz and Sabrina be passing round the mirror doing some lines.

Boo Threse goes 'Put on that ragga tape, them tunes are safe.'

Marie Turn it up I wanna get in the mood.

Boo   Deanne goes 'Don't turn it too loud that ginger hair bitch will come in here.'

Marie   They can't do nothin'.

Boo   Oy Deanne try on these shorts.

Marie   Where's the taxi meeting us?

Boo   Deniz goes 'Can anyone sort me out the fare. I'm a bit short.'

Marie   'Maybe you'll grow.'

Boo   'Tight cow.'

Marie   Uh?

Boo   Watch my lips, 'Tight cow.'

Marie   Bitch.

Boo   Don't start.

Marie   Then Deanne starts posing around in the shorts.

Boo   Gwan yard gal.

Marie   That looks wicked.

Boo   'Me arse looks fat.'

Marie   'Nah, ya arse jus' look good from far innit.'

Boo   'Me arse look good from far? How fuckin' far?'

Marie   Then she goes 'I ain't pullin' tonight anyway, I got the painters in.'

Boo   Ya on ya period?

Marie   Don't worry man just use ya gob.

Boo   Ah ya so low man.

Marie   I'm too rude.

Boo   Then Sabrina starts getting all impatient 'cos she's buzzing.

Marie   (*putting on Sabrina's voice*) 'What time ya call dis still getting ready and it's big ten o'clock, the club will be closed by the time we reach there.'

Boo   I'm trying to make her look good.

Marie   'Shall I tell the taxi to come back next year then?' 'Oy bitch, don't be coming feisty with me.'

Boo   We all pile into the taxi, Marie was sitting on my lap.

Marie sits on Boo's lap.

Boo   Don't squash me man.

Marie   Stop moanin'.

Boo   Sabrina's in the front seat and me and Deniz and Deanne and Threse are in the back.

Marie   We was pure fuckin' buzzin' innit.

Boo   Yeah. We 'ave another dab at the speed to keep the high.

Marie   Then we get the taxi driver to put a ragga station on.

Boo   Boom ska boom boom ska.

Marie   We cruise into East London and I feel light.

Boo   You ain't light.

Marie   First we go to Hackney 'cos that's where Threse know a good dealer.

Boo   The factories loom all yellow in the light.

Marie   And all the shops be boarded up looking like cages.

Boo   And the big tall flats like massive gravestones.

Marie   Hackney is a beautiful place man.

Boo   Hackney is the centre of the world.

Marie   Then we go up 'Trenz'.

Boo   People go up 'Trenz' for one thing innit. To get out their box, have a dance, and have a shag.

Marie   That's three things.

Boo   Yeah. Main one though to get out ya box.

Marie   When we reach the club I can feel the speed kicking in more. I get so horny all the men look like 'proper tings'.

Boo   A gang a' yardies being the bouncers for the night are standing around outside, seeing us come up they shout –

Marie   'Yow! Sexy! Oyoyoyo!' 'Yush man!' and we join the end of the line. If they ain't bad looking when I pass 'em I say 'Later babes.'

Boo   I'm standing next to Threse in the queue and she's starting to bring me down. She keep going on that they done murder someone in the club last week and that she come constructive and bought a blade. I just goes 'Man I ain't up for that.'

Marie   She always starts screwing on about Wendy innit.

Boo   Wendy see 'Trenz' as her cut. She reckons Threse owes her money but Threse says she already paid her and she never buy off her again 'cos she cuts the gear so it's as weak as shite. Threse always gets me proper para y' know.

Marie   She like a kid tellin' herself a story sometimes innit. She tell it again and again 'til it's true.

Boo   But none of us was up for a fight.

Marie   We was in a lovin' mood.

Boo   Ready to love them off dem mans.

A soft pounding of ragga music.

Inside the vibration of the music hit me an I feel it even in me heart.

Marie   The place was always rammed on a Friday night.

Boo   'Nuff bodies bopping and just vibesin' off the music.

Marie   And our heads be filled with the thick smell a' ganja.

Boo   Sometimes inside clubs there's so much going on I feel like out me body. Plus when the pills kick in.

Marie   It was Buju B playin'.

Boo   I see Threse pulling out her wrap and I know she be taking care a' business. Marie and Deanne was doin' their moves on the dance floor and Deniz knew the deejay so she was chattin' to him an' his crew. I didn't feel like dancing so I went up to the bar to get a drink. Across the bar from me I see Wendy and her crew clocking me. They was all dress really tatty, I was already feelin' proper para an' I must 'a looked nervous when she stare at me 'cos they move so that I had to walk past them to get back to the floor. When I'm para it ain't like I'm scared it's like a feel like I might do anything. But people look at me and think I'm scared. I bring 'nuff trouble on meself that way. I told Threse I didn't want her to deal in Wendy's face, it ain't worth it, but Threse just say 'I don't have to answer shit to any a' them.' When I walk past them I hear them say –

Marie 'Look at that lickle pickney coming down here dressed all naked and she don't know nobody.'

Boo I said 'I wouldn't touch me for nothing if I was you slag.' Then I keep going 'cos I ain't fighting them on me own when there's like six all staring evil into me back. I heard her say –

Marie 'What you ain't got that nobody got, bitch?'

Boo I turn round and stare at her face, she just turn her back like I ain't worth it.

Marie Why? Was ya scared man?

Boo I ain't seen you runnin' to fight them on ya own.

Marie There was so much heat and bodies on the dance floor. They up the volume and be playing jungle. The tunes just took control.

Boo By then I was back with all me spars again, everybody was moving – the people at the sides was nodding their heads to the music, tooting off the tables and the rage was kicking between everyone in the club.

Marie Sabrina be dancing like this.

She demonstrates some sexy moves.

Boo Deanne doing them sweet and feisty moves.

She demonstrates.

Marie Threse is jus' cool like this.

Boo And we going wild.

Marie Wine ya body gal! Nobody reach our level of krissness.

Boo Cause them nah wicked like us.

Marie Maximum style.

Boo All eyes on our posse.

Marie Everyone cussing us 'cos we so fuckin' stoosh!

Boo Itching to scratch up our faces man.

Marie 'Check how dem gals is skinning out star.'

Boo 'How can they front like that?'

Marie 'Up to them innit.'

Boo 'Them dance nasty like I don't know what.'

Marie We 'avva licence to crub like dis bitch.

Boo An' the rude bways going 'Come here sweetheart, ya a nice beef.'

Marie Gal ya too rude.

Boo I was crubbin' so 'ard I ladder me fuckin' tights.

Marie Then some geezers with nappy heads.

Boo Shabby garms, 'n' alkie breath.

Marie Be distressing our space.

Boo So we back in the toilets.

Marie Choppin' up some lines on the seats.

Boo Ra! We was buzzing, trus' me!

Marie We go back out for a second assault.

Boo Suddenly the club go quiet and there's a sound of everyone cussin' that the music had stopped . . .

Marie We come out the toilet, see everyone was crowding round the other side of the club.

Boo Threse goes 'Eh everybody's on them sides.'

Marie I heard someone say (*bored*) 'Murdah.'

Boo   There was still a few people standin' round chattin' and boppin' even tho' there weren't no music.

Marie   I heard this yard in a kangol cap go 'I thought I heard tree shots.'

Boo   Deniz goes 'Let's chip, police be here in a minute' but Threse goes . . .

Marie   'I wanna see.' Always have to be where the action is innit.

Boo   Other people are getting impatient standing around going 'Jus run dem tunes.'

Marie   'Fiver we pay.'

Boo   I keep me eye out for Marie in case we was gonna see a dead man because she has fits sometimes, don't ya, and it's only me that knows what to do. It almost used to make me feel happy when she have a fit sometimes. It make me feel happy that I know what to do. She just starts shakin' and shit and I get people's coats and put them under her. And I stroke her hair, and make every-one keep back. But she didn't have a fit that night.

Marie   We have a quick look where everyone was crowded round and I see this geezer laying on his side blood streaming out his head and mixing with the cigarette butts and shit that was on the floor.

Boo   Deanne goes 'That looked like some proper wound to me star.'

Marie   Then Wendy was by us and she say to Threse 'Yeah take a look that be you, ya come roun' here tartin' around and dealin' on this turf lickle yard gal.'

Boo   I pull Threse away 'cos I know she front it out with them otherwise but this slit-eyed woman goes 'Don't walk away bitch.' So I goes 'If we don't wanna stand round here rampin' with you whores then that's up to us.' She go 'Who you think you are bitch' then Threse goes 'You better not call her shit before I would just box you in ya face. You and all a' dem scatty prostitutes ya move with.' Wendy goes 'Ah, I been waiting for this man.' Threse goes 'I ain't afraid to fight with you ya filthy tramp' then Wendy goes –

Marie   'Good 'cos I'm gwan kill you bitch!' and she leap on her . . .

Boo   Like a animal.

Marie   Grabbin' her hair trying to slap her face. Threse grab one of her nose rings and rip it out her face and her nose rip and was dripping blood.

Boo   This woman's got my hair. I twist free and I see her standing with a lump of my hair in her hand. I don't feel, I just see it. I hear the music start up again.

Marie   They think it stops fights to put the music on.

Boo   I get up and I start singing and dancing to the music. I get a smack in the back of my head but I'm still just dancing.

Marie   You just nutty in fights man.

Boo   I don't even feel nothing. I think it's the speed. All the fear makes me go out of meself.

Marie   People are ramming out the doors as the sound of sirens fills the air.

Boo   I hear Threse go 'No-one fucks with our crew. We teach them.'

Marie   I hear Sabrina shouting 'The handcuffs are too tight' and I know the police, them come inside.

Boo   Babylon. I had two of them sitting on me. One

on my chest and one on me legs. I shout get off me but I don't think I made no sound.

Marie They took us all down the station and we spend the night in a police cell.

Boo How's my face?

Marie Same as usual, a fuckin' mess.

They drag the chairs further apart, and sit on them with their backs to each other.

Marie (*as Deniz: she begins speaking in unintelligible patois*) 'Yeah das how dey run ting in a ghetto we jus deal wi' ting up front know what me a say then poliss 'em come an make enquiry an write it ahn papah half hour dis half hour dat you know what me a say you want me say yes fit dis or yes fit dat cyan arks me in plain English I nah say a word. Wha? I'm speakin' English wish language be dis. Yeah man y' ave to check it out 'im bring a bag a gun and dem fire 'pon yout' and yout' and yout' an ya poliss frien' come for dem gun an' I tell 'em na run. Man nah stop kill man seen, man nah stop rob man seen. A' wha' gwan in de ghetto me bruddah?'

Boo Down the station I could hear Deniz in the next room doin' her Jamaican act. I already spent a lot of nights down the station before I ever commit a crime. They always question us about the yardie dealers in the area. I just act stupid. I just told them the next day was my birthday and I wanted to go home. They treated it as a lie but I was bein' real. I'd forgotten but the next day was me birthday. 'E ask me why I was so cagey and nervous. I said I ain't nervous. 'E said ya ain't nervous? Feel ya heart. And he put his hand on me heart. It don't matter how many times I end up in a police cell I 'spose I always get nervous, but you have to front it out 'cos some of them love their job. He give up questioning me and they just leave us to sleep, although I can never sleep in them places. The graffiti fucks up my mind. I kept hearing Threse in another cell going 'Let me out I need a dump.' I knew she must be up for unlawful possession of weapon, and I didn't know if she still have gear on her. I'm thinking her bail be about five hundred quid so it'd be like 'See ya later babe.' Me they jus let me off with a caution. But it was weird. In the morning Threse got a result.

Marie   What you go down on him in that room las' night or what? *(as Threse, defensively)* 'Nah man they jus' caution me is all.'

Boo   Sabrina and Deanne start prancin' about in front of her singing that 'Informer' song.

Marie   Threse kept shouting at them to fuck off. She was really red in the face. Tryin' to speech her way out of it.

Boo   Deniz goes 'Low it Threse, no-one's brushin' ya, we ya spars innit, we just sayin' don't fuck with that lot. Cross them one time we visit you in hospital the next morning.' That shut her up for once.

Marie   There was this squat we used to go to in Hackney right on the top floor of this block flats where Threse used to live. Some of the flats was vacant.

Boo   It smelt like somebody died there.

Marie   It was musty.

Boo   The squat was empty, 'cept for the blankets we had put on the floor.

Marie   Wallpaper was hanging off the wall and one of the windows was smashed. It was cold as well weren't it.

Boo   Freeze ya tits off up there.

Marie The floor was covered in pillows and chip wrappers, cans and candles we had bought.

Boo But we liked it 'cos it was ours.

Marie No-one knew where we was there.

Boo That's where we went to sleep off the night before.

Marie We was all knackered and hungry.

Boo I woke up and Marie was still asleep. I wanted to go and see Nero without her. See if he have got me anything for me birthday. But all I got from him was a lecture. I didn't feel like a lecture from him sitting in his boxer shorts with a fat belly an' flip-flops at five in the afternoon. He ask me where I been the night before so I tell him about the police. He ask me how old I was this birthday so I told him sixteen. He said 'You're young, why you getting into all this is it the money sound good to you?' I said yeah. But inside I didn't know. Things jus' happen. He said weren't I interested in getting out the area? I said 'No-one ever get out the area' but inside I just thought 'Why get out, I love Hackney man.' 'E look tired of me and I felt bad that I have tired him. He said I ain't got no hope left, the way I was going I was going to be dead or lock up before I was twenty. I said weren't he going to make love to me today? 'E look at me for a bit and then he said 'Can't ya see you're not happy.' On the way back to the flat I thought about what he said. I used to think I was unhappy. There was a time when I wanted things and that made me unhappy but I teach meself not to. When I got back to the flat it was dark outside. On the landing I smell chips and alcohol. I see the girls had got more candles and put them all around that musty room. They was all bevved up. Off their faces. They jump on me an' start singing Happy Birthday.

Marie Where ya been?

Boo   Jus' walkin'.

Marie   Oh yeah. We tief yah some alcs mate. But we ain't got no gear 'cos we all brassic.

Boo   I see ya start already.

Marie   Y' aright?

Boo   Yeah.

Marie   We got Tippex filler and glue is all.

Boo   Sounds alright.

Marie   Y' aright?

Boo   Yeah.

Marie   It's ya birthday innit.

Boo   Don't remind me. I feel 'nuff old.

Marie   Deanne goes 'Sixteen is a safe age to be. After twenty is downhill.' I goes so where ya been?

Boo   I told 'em I been to see Nero and Marie started looking at me all off key. I told 'em what he said to me.

Marie   Deniz goes 'The best way to be happy is to realise nothing don't mean shit then ya can be happy.'

Boo   This upset Deanne.

Marie   Everytin' upset Deanne.

Boo   She goes 'I still got things that mean shit to me.' She reckoned it was the gear talking when we talk like that.

Marie   I put some sounds on and we drunk some rum and started dancing. Then we done the glue. I started to get a rush that was burning my head. We all started pissing ourselves laughing and singing and dancing. Weren't it.

Boo   Deanne starts laughing, singing along to the music and getting all the words wrong.

Marie   Yeah. Then we dare you to down a whole bottle of rum. Then Threse topped the dare an' dared ya to down some rum and then jump from the balcony to the balcony of the other flats.

Boo   We was on the top floor of the block of flats and each flat had its own balcony. I open the door to the balcony and I run out and look down. Straight away the dark hit me and I puke up, the height make me feel sick. Everyone was laughin' at me when I fell back into the room.

Marie   Then Deanne went out with a bottle of rum. She put the bottle on the edge of the balcony and then she climbed up slowly.

Boo   She was wearing a tight mini skirt and she hitch it right up. She crouch on the ledge at first and Deniz shouted 'We can see ya knickers.' Then she raise herself up standing on the ledge. She was swaying unsteady. The light from the window was lighting up her face and all behind her was black. And the wind made her scream. She was just screaming going 'Yard Gal we a run t'ing.' I felt it inside, and I said out loud 'Shit she gonna kill herself' Sabrina goes 'Don't touch her man you push her off.' Deanne was laughing going 'Come up here man it's wicked' like she was lovin it, but I see her fear. She keep her feet still and her body was stiff underneath her movement. She goes 'Wine ya body gal' and she make a few moves like to dance. She lose her balance and put her hand out to catch herself. I look at Sabrina's eyes and they was wide staring. I look at Marie and her eyes was closed.

Marie closes her eyes.

37

It 'appen so fast. One minute she was laughin' and the next I see her face look scared. I see her strain as she go back and she put a hand out like we might catch her then she was gone.We just had to run back to the home or they would a question us again when the ambulance come. They said when they found her she didn't have no face. That night I couldn't sleep. I went into Marie's room but she weren't there. I was looking for you everywhere, but she was gone.

Marie   I didn't wanna see no-one, looking at their faces was freaking me out. I just wanted to get out of it again. I needed something to take the edge off things and I went to Nero's place but some other woman was there laughing at me like I was some silly little girl. I don't know why but then I felt like going to me Dad's place. I ain't seen him in a few months, and I ain't supposed to see him on my own but sometimes we was quite close. But he weren't pleased to see me. I forgot what I had on. I ain't spoke to him in like three weeks, but with everything going on in my head I forgot.

Boo   I found Marie later back in that room. Her face was mash up. I said 'Wha' happen?' but she just shook her head. I sat down next to her and put me arm round her. I started crying, I didn't know why except that she was crying.

Marie   Why did he do it?

Boo   I thought she been with a punter and I said 'They're bastards man.'

Marie   'E needs mental help.

Boo   You're alright now.

Marie   He was drunk. It was like when I was young. I could feel blood in my ears. I think he burst my ear. 'E wanted to kill me.

Boo You're alright, you're alright.

Marie What did I do to deserve him?

Boo Nothing man. Nothing.

They hug. Boo goes to let Marie go, then realises she is crying still.

Boo You OK?

Marie Yeah. It was Deanne man. We shouldn't of told them about Deanne.

Boo You wanna stop telling it?

Marie Yeah.

Boo Marie?

Marie I'll be alright . . . jus run dis ting, Boo.

Act Two

Marie sits withdrawn, as Boo continues with the story.

Boo The bright morning sunshine hit me like a slap in the face. We was walking down Camden Road to the market. Marie was dancing around in front of us saying what a beautiful day it was. She was like that one minute she could be right down and then the next she was buzzing. I been up the whole night before with Threse listenin' to her talking stupidness in me earhole. Things I don't wanna know like whose ripping off who, who owe her what and her fucking fantasies about some dealer who know a dealer who fucked off to the Bahamas. She had this idea about buying a ki of gear, cutting it to make double our money, and selling it at a profit. She said she wanted to get out the kids' home and out of Hackney. If I had three grand to buy the ki with I might of wanted to hear it. But she was always scheming things like that and going on about it. We all wanted to get out the kids' home weren't it.

Marie Yeah. (*comforting herself*) We bump into Nero. 'E give us a big hug. (*She hugs herself.*) He kiss me and when I pull back I have dope in my mouth.

Boo Threse an' that lot don't really know him and they was like 'Eurgh is that the new material ya dealing with.'

Marie Sabrina goes 'Alright grandad.' I said 'I'm sorry bout me friend.' But I was embarrassed 'cos he did look a bit dusty.

Boo He give us some weed on tick and that shut Threse and Sabrina up, and Marie said she was gonna go and see him later so I started looking at her off key, and Nero goes to Marie 'Later sweetness.'

Marie We decide we gonna look round the market and then go to a pub down the canal. We was trying on all the sunglasses at this stall when Deniz suddenly pointed across the street.

Boo Wendy's crew. She ain't wid dem.

Marie Are they looking over here?

Boo Threse goes 'Where are they?'

Marie Over there.

Boo Deniz goes 'I'll give them something to stare at.'

Marie Sabrina goes 'They keep looking at me like that I'm gwan box them up mate.'

Boo Threse started looking all uptight.

Marie She hate violence.

They laugh.

Boo She was going 'Don't look at them man, is all finish.'

Marie I goes 'The way they looking at us don't seem like is all finish to me.'

Boo Threse jus look at Marie who was trying on a cap and goes 'Move ya arse Marie, you want them to come over here.'

Marie We started walking back toward the tube.

Boo When I look around they was still in the same place looking over their shoulders at us.

Marie Sabrina wanted to go down to the canal, but Threse wanted to get out the area. Sabrina faced her down and ask her what she acting like such a cheef for.

Boo We was all getting bored of Threse being moody so we started fuckin' about and having a laugh.

Marie We started rampin' with people just to make a lot of noise.

Boo (*to a member of the audience*) Oy you, why you sitting there like you just wet yourself?

Marie Oy don't be giving us no bad looks star.

Boo We say whatever the fuck we like.

Marie And none of it don't mean shit.

Boo You just have to let everybody know you're here innit.

Marie Oy, check out my tight arse man.

Boo What you chatting about? You got a arse like a settee.

Marie (*to audience*) Fuck you man. That man you cuss showing you a bad face now.

Boo Yeah? Why don't he go home and suck his daughter's pussy some more then.

Marie (*laughing at Boo*) Shit man that was low. You're gonna get us chucked out this place.

Boo I don't care.

Marie Come over these sides Boo. Some 'a these people are 'proper ting'.

Boo I'll talk to anyone who look fit enough.

Marie I wish I was the gold tooth that be glinting between your lips man.

Boo I wish I was the boxer shorts that be hanging round ya hips.

Marie What ya think of me and Boo?

Boo We're the bollocks in't we?

Marie If someone come up to us in the street we go 'Ya ugly features is distressing me man get back.'

Boo We like to go in McDonalds innit, there was 'nuff men in there.

Marie Sabrina, she knew how to put the man dem in their place. They respec' her down to the ground innit. She was confident. She jus walk up to a man like this go 'Ya lookin' buff star.' She was like a split personality. She act totally different with the men than she did the women innit.

Boo We all did man.

Marie Then we went down to the canal and smoke up.

Boo None of us wanted to go choring, we was too relaxed.

Marie We lay on the grass and look up at the blue sky. I felt free.

Boo The surface of the canal never move. The water is all still, and I see meself in it perfectly, it make you wish that time had stopped. My head felt thick from smoking up too much. One minute I feel the sun the next minute it was like all the sound be closing in on me. Rubbish that was blowing about felt like it was running along my bones. But it was like a passing feeling, then I be back with my mates again, in a different world even tho' I hadn't moved. I sometimes feel like that where I'll be in things and then suddenly I feel out of them.

Marie Sabrina fell asleep on the grass so Threse threw her shoes in the water.

Boo Then we all fell asleep, none of us had really had much sleep lately.

Marie   When we woke up there weren't many people left on the streets.

Boo   The sun had move a bit behind the clouds and we started walking back toward the tube.

Marie   Right at the far end of the street I see Wendy's posse coming towards us.

Boo   Threse goes 'Raid!'

Marie   Wendy ain't with them.

Boo   She weren't at the market neither.

Marie   Ya reckon they been waiting for us all this time?

Boo   Maybe they went to get tooled up.

Marie   Why can't they leave us alone man?

Boo   I goes 'What did ya tell the police about Wendy, Threse?' She was all like 'Nothing.'

Marie   She goes 'If ya grass her up they be out to kill us, y' know.'

Boo   Threse was like 'I don't grass.'

Marie   They was getting quite close now.

Boo   Suddenly Sabrina goes 'Shit man you on your own,' and she started running the other way. Wendy's posse started running as well, so we all started pegging it down the street but Sabrina didn't have no shoes on and I knew if we left her there she'd get mash up bad.

Marie   I look behind me and see Wendy grab Sabrina's top and pull her down. Then I see Bukola stop and go back for her and it look like one of Wendy's gang was gonna head-butt her, so I went back and tried to knock her down, and this fat one grab my arm.

Boo All these people were crossing over to the other side of the street, and some of them was standing round but no-one did nothing. Then I heard someone say 'Shit that gal gonna cut her up.' I look up and I shouted at Marie 'Knife!' but she was already stabbed. She started fitting, shaking. And all blood was coming through her hands. Wendy's posse shout 'Gavvers' and they run. Threse run as well but I stayed with Marie. I put my arm round Marie and started shouting at all the people around us to fuck off but it seem like they was deaf or stupid or love the sight of someone cut up. They took Marie into hospital and me down the station. With all the excitement I forgot about the blow in me pockets and I got a fine. Threse was avoiding us for days then the next week she come up trying to sweet me up 'Y' alright darlin' like that. I goes 'Whass up wid you? You nuh' know say we been friends from time so I back you up but I'm sick of your shit. I dunno who ya tink y' are, ya think ya some big dealer with ya yard gal image but as soon as things get bad ya run. Ya done Marie bad man, you done her wrong. And hear this. You make me sick. You're a fucking grass and a two-faced bitch. You let us down bad man. Don't be treating people like shit or don't be crying when they turn round and do you the same way. Ya lost man. You'll 'ave no-one.' Threse fucking boxed me one.

Marie Did she?

Boo Yeah man we had a bad fight.

Marie You never told me that.

Boo It was the first time I gone against the flow and cuss her out. My face was a fucking mess. She said no-one talk to her like that and from now I better watch my back.

Marie I think it was when I was in hospital that Boo started losing it. She'd always been a bit funny.

Boo (*sarcastic*) Is it really?

Marie She kept saying she wanted me to hurry up and get out because none of our friends was there for us any more, she said she felt lost. Sabrina was avoiding us as well 'cos she had some man who was chasing her and buying her all kinds of shit. Deniz had done one of her disappearing acts and gone out on a spin. Boo had to get some money to pay her fine so she said she was grafting down the station. Picking up punters is the easiest money. But it's easier when ya with ya mates 'cos they can look after ya.

Boo When you alone you always feel like you might get attacked innit. And you always wondering what people gonna do to ya. I think you bring trouble on yaself. I dunno. But the amount of fucked up men I was pulling down the station. Men who be telling me to act like a five-year-old girl. Men who want cigarette burns in their legs. And I think I see more. When you ain't with ya mates you got your eyes open more. I used to see girls down the station. Watch them. They was younger than me. One girl I see. Clumps of her hair was missing. She look so pale and skinny she was nearly blue. I used to watch her. Something make me wonder if she got the virus. She look like AIDS on legs. Then one day I didn't see her after that.

Marie When I was in hospital they tell me I was pregnant. I was fucking gutted. I kept looking at meself in the mirror thinking I couldn't be pregnant 'cos I didn't look no different. I felt so weird. Like the baby was a alien thing inside me. I wanted it cut out. Everything felt fucked you know. I been on the gear and I couldn't remember when I last taken it. I thought 'What if the

baby is damaged?' What will I do?' It make me feel sick
to have it inside me. It make me think about my Mum
and I didn't want to think about her. I wanted to find
Boo. But I didn't know where she was. It seem like she
disappear.

Boo   I was sitting in a public loo near the station.
I woke up to find my arse hanging in the toilet bowl.
I remember I come in fuck knows how long ago to shoot
up. I splash water on my face and walk out the toilet.
I felt alone.The sun was shining again but I felt numb.
When I'd looked at myself in the mirror in the toilet
I looked like shit. I had dark rings under my eyes and
I had all spots round my chin. I looked like a junkie.
The weeks when Marie was in hospital and all my mates
was avoiding me was the longest of my life. I stopped
going to see Marie. I was doing stupid shit like grafting,
pulling punters, then spending all my money getting off
my head and lying in the roads on me own. I swear to
God I used to lie in the road and cars had to drive around
me until someone drag me out the way. I weren't doing
uppers anymore like when I was with my mates. I was
doing all the downers I could get hold of – valium, brown,
booze, everything just to keep me head still. On the
street you go up or you go down. I felt like I needed
to stand still for a while but I didn't know where to go.
I felt like somebody had to understand what was inside
of me or I was gonna flip. I tried to phone Nero but his
phone was switched off. I think he had enough of me
anyway.

Marie   I couldn't find Boo. I went down the station
to score, my head was so confused I needed to talk to
someone or get some gear. I see Threse. I was trying
to pull meself together so she wouldn't know how
desperate I was for the gear. I went up behind her and
I goes 'Alright.' She took ages to turn round and finish

talking to the yards she was with. She was fucking with my head already and she ain't even spoke to me yet. She was all careless when she turn round like 'Oh Marie.' She ain't seen me since the fight. She goes 'Look at you man.' I goes 'I'm alright as it goes' She was trying to play games with me but I could see in her eyes she was pleased to see me. Threse needed the posse more than any of us. I ask Threse if she seen Boo and she said no, so we decided to go up 'Trenz' and look for her. In the taxi Threse kept going on to the yards about the day of the fight with Wendy's posse. She was turning it into something else saying how Wendy had threatened all of us and that she had tried to get us to leave the market but none of us would listen to her. I just let her tell herself them stories, if she can live with her own lies then it's up to her innit. This yard was going 'Dis Wendy sound like a proper bitch.' Threse was going 'Yeah man,' and I heard she got off with a fine after the police pick her up. I tell ya next time I see her I'm gonna be prepared man. Me and Marie are gonna fuckin' kill her in't we. I just goes yeah as in 'Yeah yeah.' She kept on getting more excited. 'We're gonna fuck her up. No-one mess with our posse and diss them like that.' I just needed to fund Boo.

Boo I went to the flat where we used to go. The place was totally empty and smelt musty. I went out onto the balcony and I stood looking at where Deanne had stood before she died. I thought about Deanne a lot. Sometimes I wonder if she knew what she was doing when she jump that night. I felt sick when I look over the balcony. Everything looked so normal. People just walking and going about their business. I went down and lay in the road where she fell. I call for Marie, but she never come.

Marie When we got to 'Sounz' Boo weren't there. We had a few drinks. Then Threse said she wanted to show me something so we went in the toilet. She took out this massive bundle of money from her knickers. I was like 'Shit where did you get that from?' She said it didn't matter, what mattered was what she was gonna use it for. I goes 'To get out?' She said 'No.' Why should she be the one to run? It was gonna be Wendy who was gonna be the one to run. She said she was gonna off Wendy. She was gonna buy a gat with the money and blow her fucking tits off. I wanted to use the money to get an ounce. Threse said we'd use some of it for the ounce but there was this geezer she knew, one of the bouncers at the 'Trenz' club who'd offered her a gat on the black market. So we decided to go up 'Trenz'.

Boo   I been following this geezer trying to nick this money. I see him took out the cashpoint on Mare Street. I was all the way out near Clapton and I had to walk back to the Amhurst Road. All the time I was walking I had to force meself. Something inside me felt like I was going the wrong way. But I kept going. I wanted to find Marie.

Marie   Up 'Trenz' it was the usual scene. Yardies be posing around in their gear and sloshers clinging on their arms. Threse went straight up to this guy in a string vest and baggy jeans, and I see them talking and gesturing like two birds around a bit of bread. She come back up to me and goes that we have to meet him back outside in a hour. I goes 'Did ya give him the money.' She goes 'Yeah,' I goes. 'You fool.' She started looking all hyped with the effort of trying to pretend everything was cool. I was fucked off with Threse. We could have use the money for gear an now we'd never see it again. She goes 'E had to take the money to give a cut to the guy whose supplying.' I goes 'Yeah whatever Threse you'll never see it again.' She was all 'Don't be treating me like a fool Marie. I know what I'm fucking doing' I said 'Yeah yard gal,' so she goes 'So what ya saying?' I goes 'I'm saying you wouldn't know how to off a baby in a push-chair let alone a case like Wendy.' Just then Sabrina and Deniz come up screaming 'Rude Gals!' Everyone was on uppers and we's all jumping around like we ain't seen each other for years. Sabrina goes 'So what ya saying?' and Threse goes 'Marie's gonna glass Wendy.' Sabrina looked at me and I goes 'That's right.' Then I look at the front of the club and I felt this excitement – 'cos now it was said I realise I was gonna do it. They was all like 'Shit yard gal' and I kept fronting it out. Threse goes 'You said it you gotta do it now' but to me she just sounded like a silly little girl.

Boo   When I finally got to 'Trenz' I thought some of the girls might be outside but I couldn't see no-one. The music was thumping through the walls and the place sounded like it was kicking. As usual it was choka so I queued up thinking I might be paying a fiver and not find no-one. Then I decided I didn't care. I had to find Marie. I had to talk to someone. I suddenly started feeling like what if she's in a police cell somewhere and she's gwan lock up. But then I thought someone would have told me by now. I was feeling shaky. I ain't felt right since I been on the street. I looked up at the sky and it was cloudless. I had another rush like a feeling that I had to get out of this place.

Marie   All the music and the lights was going through my body. People kept knocking into me but I didn't feel it. My heart was racing from the uppers. Threse's face was all lit up by the red lights and she goes 'over on the other side' and I look over and see them all standing with some ugly geezer in a ripped shell suit. Wendy had a mouth wide laughin' at something like it's the last joke on earth. Threse goes 'You gonna do her in't ya, you said you will,' but I weren't listening. I just kept my eyes

set on them. Threse didn't have to worry. I was already
set in my mind. As I was walking towards her it felt like
the world was drunk. Like the room was tipping up.
I had to stare at her to keep my balance. The sounds in
the club was one minute really loud then really soft, like
a sea. I felt sort of tall and like my hand was swelling up
round the glass I was holding. I heard Sabrina saying to
Threse 'She's a nutter' behind me, but I didn't feel they
was nothing to do with me any more. It's like part of my
mind went to this place that said I's the only person in
the world again. Threse was going 'Don't let me down
man' but I wished she'd leave me alone. I remember
being a few feet from the group. I remember Wendy
turning round and looking right into my eyes. I think she
step back and say 'No don't' but I was out of it I can't
remember. I put the glass in her neck. I turned it and see
her flesh go white. I heard her scream but then I realise
the scream had come from her mate. Blood was coming
from her neck like a waterfall. Everyone was backing
away from her. She was lumbering around holding her
neck like there was a scorpion on it. Then she fell to the
ground. I see the guy in the shell suit looking down like
he was worried he had blood on his clothes. Then I turn
and I remembered I should run, I heard Threse go 'You
know now them who test Threse will feel pain.' Boo was
standing there looking at me like a child. I push her and
shout 'Ruuun' in her face. She dropped her drink and
I see her back and the 'Moschino' sign on her shirt
pushing through the bodies. The rain had stopped outside and it was dark. The music in the club kept going.
People been glassed there every week. I lost the others
inside I come out the fire exit on my own. I finally see
them in the car park. They was all speeching over each
other except for Boo who was quiet. They was arguing
about where to go next where we should hide out and
who see us. Then Sabrina started cussing me saying

I shouldn't have gone for her neck I was only s'posed to go for her face and now they all be up for a murder charge. Threse who was always going on about being a pussy and being a chicken was shitting bricks. Part of my mind felt afraid for myself. Part of my mind didn't care. I told them all to 'low it. I said they'd all wanted her dead. Threse started speechin' me back so I just told her to fuck off and get out my face and run home. She said she ain't gonna be my co-d, if that's what I thought, but I weren't listening no more. They goes 'Come on Bukola' because she was the only one that weren't walking away but Boo stayed.

Boo   Everything was silent between me and Marie. I was shivering and she give me her jacket. It had blood on. I just said 'Nothing'll be the same now.' Then I goes 'Wha' happen man. What you on?' She was crying. She goes 'I don't know.' Then she told me she's pregnant. When I see the blue lights in the distance I said 'You better go.' She goes 'I don't want to.' So I shout in her face 'RUN.' She look at me like she don't understand. She look at me like she's hurt. And then she run . . . fast, then faster. The next time I hear from her I's inside.

Act Three

Boo drags her chair slightly apart from Marie.

Boo Friends are the people who wanna take care of
you and you wanna take care of them innit. I never
thought if I went down it would be by one of my mates
grassing me. But I know it weren't Marie. It was Threse.
She hate me since that fight. The only way she see a
friend is someone who agrees with her, and hypes her up.
Otherwise watch your back. Sometimes I think about the
girls on the outside and what they doing. Smoking up,
doing their crime, getting fucked drinking and dossing
innit. Probably waking up going that they're bored. Man
they should come in 'ere then they know what bored is.
In here I got mates but it ain't the same. I smoke enuff
weed with everyone and chat and that but here everyone
is wanting to get in ya business. Just 'cos they bored.
And they wanna stir it and make trouble for you to 'ave
power over you. They think they know and they don't,
ya know? Sometimes I play games with meself in my cell.
I got a little window that looks at the block opposite me.
Sometimes I count all the windows in the opposite block
and I divide it by the time I got left and I think how all
of us was doing the same time we'd be out tomorrow
but we ain't, we're all doing our own time. I got twenty-
three months left. I only been here a month and it's
already doing my head in. They said it was 'wounding,
with malicious intent'. I got two years. Everything went
silent in my head. I felt the world was silent when they
told me. But I fronted it out. 'Do ya bird' is what they
say. I'll do it standing on my head. Marie said she'll stick
by me but she's full of shit. She said she'll come and visit

but she don't. I don't even know if she think of me or if she leave me in here to rot. But I miss Marie you know. I think about her and I even worry about her sometimes. I think about what if she has a fit and I ain't there. I think about what if she's out by herself. I even want to tell her 'Don't go out by yourself.' Who's gonna look after her? On the street people will walk away or mug her. When I get out I'm gonna find her even though she ain't been to visit me. I thought she would. But I still find her when I get out. She's my friend from time. My best friend. Yeah Marie. You're nice. Yesterday I wrote Marie a letter:

'Dear Marie,

'I heard you phone and ask for me number. I'm in fucking prison man you can't be telling the screws to get me they ain't fuckin' British Telecom. Eight o'clock means in my room banged up. Can ya write to me and tell me what's going on? I jus wanna hear about wha's happenin' outside or visit me. Why ain't you come visit me man?

'In here it's fucking rules everywhere. I change me sheets every day and go for medicine twice a day. I get so many pills man. Everyone else is gone and I'm still sitting by the trolley trying to down them all. In here I get tablets for being a paranoid schizophrenic. You always knew I's a nutter didn't ya?

'The screws in here you can't tell if they're men or women. Some of the screws are alright as it goes. If I'm stressed out they'll come and chat to me, have a laugh, sometimes they'll even give me a proper fag. But some of 'em love their fucking keys. How sad innit.

'When I think about that night at 'Trenz' you was so fucking gone. There was more people there who could have stop you. But they egg you on. I know if I was there I would have stop you.

'I miss you Marie why ain't you come and visit me?
'Love Boo.'

54

Marie   'Dear Boo,

'I'm sorry I ain't been to see ya. I got no money I swear. It's hard man – I'm trying to get the flat the council give me together but it's still a dump. Sometimes I imagine you standing at the door going "Marie man sort dis place what's goin' on in this gaff?"

'I ain't wrote. I didn't think you'd even wanna speak to me from that night. If I say I'm sorry I just feel like I'm taking the piss. I'm gonna come see you though.

I went down the job centre today. I wait for me number to be call. Most of the jobs they want people with experience though, I ain't got nothin'. They got some doing hairdressing. I dunno why I was looking at them because I can't even do me own. They ask me to fill in a form. I was shaking when I tell her I couldn't write. I wanted just to run out. Even in interviews me mind keeps floating off. I can't understand what they saying. Sometimes I get a panicky feelin' like I wanna run out the room. It's hard being sober man. I don't wanna be like everyone else and just be living for the next day. I dunno what I want.'

Boo   'Dear Marie,

'We haunt some low places but job interviews, I never think ya go so low. We been on bang up this weekend. Lock us up like animals. With a shit pan in the corner I got a crouch and do me shit and sleep with it in me fuckin' cell 'til morning. Can you believe that Marie? I was howling like a dog by Sunday. Thought I was going off me head. If they treat me like an animal I will be an animal. Ooooooooow. I started pretending I have a illness or something shouting "Nurse, nurse" but they don't fucking hear me. I smash up me cell so I'm on report now. Ya still ain't come to visit me Marie.'

Marie and Boo sit opposite each other as if they were on a visit. The atmosphere is awkward.

Marie   So how ya doing?

Boo   How am I doing? I'm like you see, in' I?

   Pause.

Marie   What the girls like in here?

Boo   Alright. Some of them are more than alright. How's everyone?

Marie   Don't see them that much. Now and then.

Boo   Fuckin' and fightin' as usual I suppose.

   Pause.

Is it true Threse gone bang up?

Marie   I dunno. Yeah I heard that.

Boo   If she did I'm glad.

   Pause.

Marie   Next time I come in ya want me to bring ya some clothes?

Boo   Why ya got too much money at the moment?

Marie   Why, ya bein' so cold man?

Boo   Took ya time coming to see me didn't ya?

Marie   I could bring ya some gear next time I come in.

Boo   Nah. I ain't getting back on the gear 'til I get out. Then I'm gonna kill it.

Marie   I've kicked.

Boo   Yeah?

Marie   Yeah.

Boo   That's good.

Marie   But I still bring ya anything ya want.

Boo   Don't worry about it. If I want gear I get it free in here. Don't need to go begging to you.

Marie   You've become really bitter since you been in here you know that.

Boo   (*explosive*) So why ya came and visit me?

Marie   I'm only trying . . .

Boo   (*almost shouting*) AND I'M ONLY 'TRYING' . . .

Having been full of rage Boo is suddenly calm.

Marie   Shit.

Boo   You look different.

Marie   So do you.

Boo   You've put on weight.

Marie   Yeah.

Boo   You still looking for a job?

Marie   I'm gonna wait 'til after the baby.

Boo   Is it? You looking forward to the baby?

She nods.

Marie   You gonna look for a job when you get out?

Boo   (*laughs*) I dunno. A job. I'm wondering how I'm gonna feel just walking down the street. How it will be just to walk. That feels like it's never gonna happen. I can't imagine it anyway.

Marie   Don't think like that Boo.

Boo shrugs.

Marie   You can live with me you know when you get out.

Boo Thanks.

Pause.

What you gonna call the baby?

Marie I'm thinking about a Nigerian name.

Boo Yeah?

Marie Yeah.

They laugh.

Bus leaves in eight minutes.

Boo You better go.

Marie Yeah. I wanna say something more.

Boo Nothing more to say is there.

Marie I'll be back.

Boo Yeah.

They face the audience again, sitting apart.

Marie In the end Boo never come live with me. She stop writing to me a few months before she come out. I been sending her letters trying to big her up like.

'Dear Boo,
    'Today I took little Bukola for a walk with the pram to the park. I was all in me jays and feelin' down. I started to feed the ducks but they chase me. Imagine me in the park wiv me bag of bread runnin' from the ducks with me pram. Them ducks was feisty man. Boo is really pretty now she a month old. She used to look scary with her little face so angry but now she's sweet. I wish you could see her. Sometimes I feel lonely though. But then I was thinking about where I was this time last year. Even tho' it's hard I'm thinking how I got a flat now. And I sort of got a family. If I can stay away from the

gear. I 'ave to talk meself out of the gear all the time man. I thought it would change when I have a baby. But life gets harder I think. Sometimes I think about Deanne. An' I start talking to meself to stay away from the drugs. I know once I start that's it. I wanna get meself together for Boo. When you get out I want you to come and live with us as well. You always look out for me Boo. Now I wanna do the same for you. Please write to me, I miss you.

'Love Marie.'

I dunno where Boo went to, I never hear from anyone who know her. I hope I see her again on the outside. Some people. They stay inside you. I dunno why. She's a mate, you know. She's always somewhere in my mind, always with me, all the time. I dunno where she go when she got out, but I miss her for time.

Boo I don't think they should lock people away ya know. I ain't even nineteen and I feel like me life is sorted for me. I dunno how I'll feel when I get out. I think I'll feel lonely and lost. I'll try and find my own direction. But I think it will be hard. I think about not having my number. GJ0664. It feels like in the distance. Never. I wonder who will have my cell after me. I think about Marie you know. I'm glad she was my friend. But I need to get away from all that scene and people who knew me. Every one you known stays inside you a bit don't they. I'm on my own from now. But she was my friend. My best friend.

Marie From time.

Boo From time.

Marie Can we go now?

Boo Can we go?